TEEN LIFE

I HAVE ADD/ADHD.
NOW WHAT?

NICKI PETER PETRIKOWSKI

ROSEN
PUBLISHING®

New York

Published in 2016 by The Rosen Publishing Group, Inc.
29 East 21st Street, New York, NY 10010

First Edition

Library of Congress Cataloging-in-Publication Data

Petrikowski, Nicki Peter.
I have ADD/ADHD. Now what?/Nicki Peter Petrikowski.—
First edition.
        pages cm.—(Teen life 411)
Includes bibliographical references and index.
Audience: Grade 7–12
ISBN 978-1-4994-6144-2 (library bound)
1. Attention-deficit disorder in adolescence—Popular works.
I. Title.
RJ506.H9P49 2016
616.85'8900835—dc23

                                        2014044181

Manufactured in the United States of America

CONTENTS

Everybody finds it difficult sometimes to concentrate and finish an assignment. This is especially the case when working on something that you have to do but that does not seem all that interesting. There are many possible things that make it hard to focus or lead to a person being easily distracted. Among many other things, lack of sleep, a reaction to something you ate, being worried about something, or being infatuated with someone may hamper your concentration and cause your mind to wander.

But what if this is something that does not only happen to you occasionally but over a long period of time? What if you are constantly distracted, inattentive, and forgetful and regularly have trouble getting tasks done? What if there are no outside factors that could explain it? If that is the case, it may point to a neurological condition known as attention-deficit/hyperactivity disorder, or ADHD for short.

ADHD is the most common psychiatric disorder school age children are diagnosed with in the United States. According to the National Resource Center on ADHD, 5 to 8 percent of all children are affected, and some estimates are even higher.

ADHD has attracted a lot of attention in recent years, not only by medical specialists but also by the media. Since this condition was virtually unknown a relatively short time ago, its current prevalence has been cause for controversy. Some people even

Consistently being unable to concentrate while studying could be a sign that you have attention-deficit/hyperactivity disorder.

go so far as to claim that ADHD is not a real condition but made up by the pharmaceutical industry to sell their drugs, which was adopted by parents looking for a way to deal with the behavior of a young person seen as difficult.

Anybody affected by ADHD knows that these claims are nonsense, and their experience is backed up by science. ADHD is very real, and it has a marked effect not only on the lives of those diagnosed with it but also on their families and friends. It has an impact on relationships, on the development of social skills, on school performance, and on self-esteem.

While there is no cure for ADHD at this point, there are treatment options available that help manage the symptoms. This includes medication, which affects chemicals in the brain to allow those taking it to be more focused. It also includes therapy to practice required skills and learn useful techniques for becoming more organized and more productive.

If you have ADHD, it will play a big part in your life. But it will only control your life if you let it. You can take charge of your condition, and the best first step is to get informed.

CHAPTER 1

Attention-deficit disorder (ADD) or, as it is now more commonly referred to, attention-deficit/hyperactivity disorder (ADHD) is a behavioral disorder most commonly diagnosed in young children, although in some cases it is discovered at a later age.

As the name implies, those who have ADHD often have difficulty paying attention and focusing on a task. They are easily distracted and they find it hard to get back to their work once their concentration has been broken. This is not always the case, though, and usually it is only a problem when dealing with something the individual with ADHD is not really interested in. If the person is interested, he or she can concentrate on something intently, sometimes too intently. Being so focused on an activity that you forget everything else around you is called hyperfocus.

Hyperactivity is a symptom often observed in children diagnosed with ADHD, but once they reach their teenage years, this tends to lessen. However, adolescents and adults with ADHD often suffer from restlessness and may find it difficult to sit still. The symptoms and their severity differ from case to case.

Individuals with ADHD often have problems in school because their inattentiveness makes it hard to keep up. It can be very

People with ADHD get distracted easily. The disorder may be more prevalent today because we have more sources of distraction.

frustrating to fail despite trying hard and, in the worst case, to be labeled as lazy or stupid although that is not true. There is no link between ADHD and the intelligence of the person suffering from it.

While there is no cure at this point, ADHD can be treated. Medication and therapy can help deal with the symptoms. If it is not treated correctly, the affected individual is at risk of failing school and having difficulties with relationships and with keeping a job and might even end up having trouble with the law. It's not all bad, though. While ADHD causes problems for those affected, they typically have strengths and positive qualities as well.

A smartphone puts a world of information and entertainment into the palm of your hand, but this constant availability has drawbacks as well.

People with ADHD are often especially creative, capable of thinking outside the box, spontaneous, and forgiving, and they tend to have a strong sense of justice.

CAUSES

The exact causes of ADHD are not clearly understood at this point, but it is clear that genetics play a part. Studies have shown that ADHD is hereditary. In other words, the child of a person with ADHD is likely to have ADHD as well, and specific genes that apparently are involved have been identified. The genes can't be the only factor, though, which is apparent when looking at twins. Although they share the same genetic material, one twin having ADHD does not necessarily mean that the other has it, too, although the likelihood is very high (upwards of 80 percent). This proves that some people have a genetic predisposition for developing ADHD, but that something else must play a part as well.

Hence a wide range of environmental factors are also considered. Low birth weight or premature birth are thought to have an influence, as does the exposure to lead (such as in paint). ADHD seems to be more likely to affect children whose mothers smoked or drank alcohol during pregnancy, but it is uncertain whether this is a cause or correlation. Seeing as how the mother of a young person with ADHD is more likely to have ADHD herself, she is also more likely to suffer from a lack of self control. This in turn raises the chances that she would smoke or drink while pregnant. Other outside factors that have often been suspected like (allegedly) bad parenting, food additives like artificial food coloring, or too much refined sugar have been ruled out as possible causes.

Brain imaging studies have shown that the brain of a person with ADHD develops differently than that of a person without ADHD. Some parts of the brain concerned with self-regulation are a bit smaller in children with ADHD compared to children of the same age. Also, certain brain chemicals responsible for carrying information between the nerves in the parts of the brain regulating behavior function abnormally.

While the brain of a young person with ADHD follows a normal pattern of development, it takes three years longer on average until it reaches peak thickness and fully matures compared to the brain of a young person without the condition. So while it lags behind, it still catches up eventually, which could be the explanation why certain symptoms of ADHD diminish when a young person with ADHD gets older.

THE DIFFERENT TYPES OF ADD/ADHD

The *Diagnostic and Statistical Manual of Mental Disorders (DSM)*, published by the American Psychiatric Association, is a handbook listing hundreds of psychiatric disorders and the criteria for their diagnosis. It describes three different subtypes of ADHD, depending on the symptoms shown: the predominantly inattentive representation, the predominantly hyperactive-impulsive representation, and the combined representation.

Someone with the predominantly inattentive type of ADHD will have difficulty focusing on something. Sometimes these individuals are described as dreamers who get easily distracted instead of concentrating on a task. They tend to forget things, even something they were told mere moments ago. They are also prone to make careless mistakes as they find it difficult to pay attention to details.

This representation of ADHD is sometimes diagnosed later in life because it may not cause any severe problems for years and only become apparent once performance at school or at work begins to suffer. It is also more common in females than it is in males. This subtype is sometimes referred to as attention-deficit disorder (ADD) to differentiate it from the other types of the disorder. This makes sense considering that hyperactivity is not a symptom. In technical terminology, the name ADD is outdated though.

The predominantly hyperactive-impulsive type of ADHD on the other hand is apparent from a young age, as a young person with this condition seems to be moving constantly. It is difficult for them to remain seated, and when they have to they usually fidget or squirm in their seat or tap their foot constantly. They have a tendency to run around, climbing and touching things, while being unable to play or work quietly.

This usually lessens with age, turning into an inner restlessness.

Not everybody who has ADHD shows signs of hyperactivity. Some are naturally quiet and introspective dreamers.

Impulsiveness means acting without thinking and being unable to wait, be it in a line or waiting for your turn in a game. Blurting out an answer before the question has been asked in full or butting into other people's conversations are also signs of it. This type of ADHD is diagnosed a lot more rarely than the other two.

The combined representation is the most common type of ADHD, which shows symptoms of both the inattentive and the hyperactive-impulsive representations.

The *DSM* is used as a standard reference in the United States and many other places. Another such diagnostic tool is the *International Classification of Diseases* (*ICD*), maintained by the World Health Organization. The *ICD* refers to ADHD as hyperkinetic disorder. The guidelines for a diagnosis are stricter in the *ICD* than they are in the *DSM*, as the individual has to show symptoms of inattentiveness, hyperactivity, and impulsiveness. According to the *DSM*, symptoms from one of these three areas can be enough. This is likely a reason why the percentage of people diagnosed with the disorder is lower in Europe where the *ICD* is used as reference compared to the United States.

A Short History of ADD/ADHD

Attention-deficit/hyperactivity disorder was first recognized as a mental disorder in 1968. The American Psychiatric Association included it in its second edition

ADHD is a controversial topic, and there are many factors contributing to that. The cause is not fully identified yet. There is no simple test for it. A standardized method of assessment does not exist. The diagnosis relies on the judgment of a doctor and is therefore subjective; different physicians may come to different conclusions. And since just about everybody shows similar symptoms at one point or another, it is difficult to draw the line between normal behavior and this disorder.

Some critics claim that ADHD does not exist. They blame it on environmental factors like bad parenting, too much sugar in their diet, too much television, or various other things. Some claim that the condition was invented by pharmaceutical companies to sell their drugs, and that parents gladly jumped at the chance to sedate their unruly children.

Most of these claims stem from blatant ignorance. Historical sources make clear that the condition is older than the drugs it was allegedly invented to sell. And scientific studies have ruled out many formerly suspected causes. Instead, they point to a biological origin of the disorder. Some environmental factors may have an influence, but it seems clear at this point that ADHD is at least in part an issue of genetics. As far as the scientific community is concerned, there is no controversy.

Because of the subjective nature of the diagnosis, there is the risk of a patient being over-diagnosed and over-medicated. As problematic as it may be in individual cases, that has little meaning concerning the existence of the condition as a whole. Physicians can make mistakes, but it is possible to get a second opinion to minimize that risk. Unlike unfounded claims that ADHD does not exist, further research will only increase the chance that those affected will be able to get the help they need.

CONTROVERSIAL TOPIC

of the *Diagnostic and Statistical Manual of Mental Disorders* (*DSM-II*), then under the name of hyperkinetic reaction of childhood. In the *DSM-III*, published in 1980, the name was changed to attention-deficit disorder, and two subtypes of ADD were described: ADD with hyperactivity, and ADD without hyperactivity. In 1987, the distinction between the two subtypes was removed and the name changed to attention-deficit/hyperactivity disorder. This name is still in use today. The *DSM-IV*, published in 2000, added the distinction between the three subtypes described previously.

Does that mean the condition did not exist prior to 1968? That seems highly unlikely. In fact, we know of several physicians who described conditions similar to those of what we know as ADHD far earlier than that.

In 1798, Sir Alexander Crichton, a Scottish physician, published "An Inquiry into the Nature and Origin of Mental Derangement. Comprehending a Concise System of the Physiology and Pathology of the Human Mind. And a History of the Passions and their Effects." In the second book of this work, he describes a condition he refers to as "incapacity of attending with a necessary degree of constancy to any one object," with which some people are born, but which generally diminishes as they get older.

Another famous example appeared in the German children's book *Der Struwwelpeter*, which portrayed misbehaving children. It was written by psychiatrist Heinrich Hoffmann and was first published in 1845. One of the tales included, "The Story of Fidgety Phil," describes a

Control Subject   ADHD Subject

Tests have shown that some areas of the brain of a person with ADHD develop differently compared to people without ADHD.

young boy who is unable to sit still at the dinner table, causing family conflict. There is also a story about a boy showing symptoms of inattention, "Johnny Look-in-the-Air." While Hoffmann's book is hardly a medical treatise, the similarities to children diagnosed with ADHD are so striking that in Hoffmann's native Germany they are often

Die Geſchichte vom Zappel-Philipp.

„Ob der P h i l i p p heute ſtill
Wohl bei Tiſche ſitzen will?"
Alſo ſprach in ernſtem Ton
Der Papa zu ſeinem Sohn,
Und die Mutter blickte ſtumm
Auf dem ganzen Tiſch herum.
Doch der Philipp hörte nicht,
Was zu ihm der Vater ſpricht.
Er gaukelt
Und ſchaukelt,
Er trappelt
Und zappelt
Auf dem Stuhle hin und her.
„Philipp, das mißfällt mir ſehr!"

Tales such as *The Story of Fidgety Phil* may disprove claims that ADHD did not exist until recently.

referred to as "Zappelphilipp" (i.e., Fidgety Phil).

British pediatrician Sir George Frederic Still held a series of lectures titled "On Some Abnormal Psychical Conditions in Children" in 1902, in which he described twenty children suffering from what he referred to as "an abnormal defect of moral control" that had not been caused by physical disease or a lack of intelligence. Some of the symptoms Still names are similar to the impulsivity and problems with delayed gratification often observed in children diagnosed with ADHD. While it is clear that Still also described other conditions, many present-day authors consider his lectures to be the starting point for scientific research of the condition we know as ADHD.

Descriptions of behavior typical for people with ADHD in sources far older than these suggest that the disorder has affected people for thousands of years, quite possibly through all of human history, even though it is unscientific to diagnose someone based on a written account. One thing is certain, though: claims that the condition has been invented in recent years by the pharmaceutical industry are false.

MYTH

ADHD is the result of bad parenting..

FACT

Some behaviors shown by children and adolescents with ADHD may seem like the result of bad manners or rudeness. But the root for this is not a lack of discipline but brain chemistry, which can be altered.

MYTH

You can outgrow ADHD. Adults don't have it.

FACT

Maybe this myth has its roots in the fact that the symptoms of hyperactivity decline over time. Though the symptoms may change, ADHD is a lifelong condition that can have a severe negative impact on a person's life if left untreated. It is possible to learn how to manage the symptoms, though, and many people suffering from the disorder lead happy and productive lives.

MYTH

Somebody with ADHD will never amount to anything.

FACT

Many kids with ADHD have difficulties in school, but that is not because they are lazy or stupid. Also, it certainly does not mean they cannot be successful. Certain typical characteristics like creativity and the willingness to take risks may even help with that. There are many famous, high-achieving individuals who had (or have) ADHD.

CHAPTER 2

YOUR DIAGNOSIS AND TREATMENT OPTIONS

ADHD is a complex issue. This means the diagnosis and the treatment are complex as well. The condition differs from person to person, which can make the diagnosis difficult, and treatment to manage the symptoms has to be tailored to the individual. Someone who suffers from the inattentive type of ADHD has different needs than someone with the hyperactive-impulsive type. Also, the severity of certain symptoms will influence the treatment plan proposed by your doctor.

For a proper diagnosis doctors have to take the time to talk to and get to know their patients.

DIAGNOSIS

Since ADHD is such a complex and complicated issue, there is no simple way to tell whether someone has it or not. Unlike other medical problems where an X-ray or a blood test may give you a quick answer, the diagnosis relies on a complete evaluation by a health care professional.

This often involves a primary care doctor, but sometimes the expertise of a specialist like a psychiatrist or a psychologist is required. This professional will determine if there is a pattern of symptoms and whether these behaviors are more severe and more persistent than what is typical.

As mentioned before, many people suffer from some of these symptoms at some point. So for a diagnosis of ADHD, a person needs several of them to have occurred for more than six months, for them to occur in at least two settings (such as at home and at school), and to rule out other causes they could be attributed to, such as an illness or stress at home.

If it is to be as thorough as it needs to be, such an evaluation takes time, sometimes months. It likely involves talking to and observing the person with suspected ADHD. It also involves tests for intelligence and attention, as well as the involvement of parents and teachers or other people who have regular contact with the individual in question. The older the patient is, the more they should be involved. While it may be difficult for young children to do so, teenagers can describe their own situation and help their doctor figure out what the problem is.

If the doctor makes a diagnosis after only a short time, maybe even after the first appointment, it is advisable to be skeptical and maybe seek a second opinion. The reason is that ADHD is too complex to be diagnosed reliably that quickly.

Boys are about three times as likely to be diagnosed with ADHD as girls are. This may be because girls are more likely to suffer from inattentiveness rather than hyperactivity, which means their condition is less apparent and therefore presumably less often identified correctly.

Treatment

Once the diagnosis has been made, a treatment plan can be devised, which will help reduce the symptoms. There are three different options for treating ADHD: the behavioral approach, the pharmacological approach, and a combination of the two, called the multimodal approach.

The Behavioral Approach

One way to address ADHD is through therapy. This is not only for the individual suffering from the disorder but possibly also for parents and other family members. The goal is to help everybody affected to understand the condition. It is also designed to teach them ways to deal with the problems it causes.

There are other conditions that have symptoms similar to those of ADHD and can therefore be easily mistaken for it. But since different conditions require different treatment, the cause of the symptoms has to be identified so that the individual in question can get the help he or she needs.

Both below-average and above-average intelligence can lead to a person being inattentive or acting out, either because the person is overwhelmed or unchallenged. ADHD is not linked to intelligence. In other words, it is possible for someone with the disorder to be gifted or to be mentally retarded, but having ADHD is no indication of a person's intellectual capabilities.

Hearing problems can have the same effect as it is difficult to pay attention to instructions if you simply do not hear them. Low blood sugar can also be the cause of a lack of concentration, hyperactivity, and aggression. Both epilepsy and Tourette's syndrome can cause unusual behavior, which could be interpreted as symptoms of ADHD.

The inability to create emotional bonds shown by people with autism can look similar to the difficulties some individuals with ADHD have with social skills, and hyperactivity (in stimulating environments) is a symptom shared by both disorders. Stress can also lead to behavior similar to that shown by people with ADHD.

The treating physician has to consider all possible causes for the symptoms shown, which makes the diagnosis difficult, especially since it is not only possible for a person to suffer from more than one condition but likely in the case of ADHD.

SIMILAR SYMPTOMS, DIFFERENT CONDITIONS

Not everyone who seems distracted has ADHD. Inattentiveness may be a symptom of another condition.

A counselor's advice can be a great help not only for the person with ADHD, but for the whole family.

For parents, it is extremely important to understand that their child with ADHD is not being difficult on purpose but acting in a way that is natural for the child, although it may be frustrating for them. With help from a specialist, the family can learn to communicate more effectively and how to use management techniques to cope with ADHD. These techniques include creating daily routines and removing disruptive elements and helping the diagnosed person to adjust their behavior. Since individuals with the disorder have problems structuring their work and their life in general, it can be helpful to set and strictly enforce boundaries when they

ADHD often is not the only condition an affected individual is suffering from. Roughly two thirds of the people diagnosed with ADHD also have one or more coexisting conditions, also referred to as comorbidities. These related problems, which can make the diagnosis of ADHD more difficult, need to be identified and addressed by a specialist.

About half of those who have ADHD also suffer from a learning disability such as dyslexia (difficulty with reading) or dyscalculia (difficulty doing math), making success in school even more difficult.

Oppositional defiant disorder (ODD) and the more severe conduct disorder (CD) are also common coexisting conditions. The former is diagnosed in about 40 percent of children with ADHD and is characterized by a pattern of angry and defiant behavior. These include being stubborn and confrontational, breaking rules, and fits of temper. The latter affects about a quarter of the children diagnosed with ADHD. It is characterized by hostile and antisocial behavior like destroying things and being aggressive and deceitful toward other people.

Males are more likely to suffer from these externalizing disorders than females. Females are more frequently affected by internalizing disorders like depression or anxiety disorder. The symptoms of depression include losing interest in things you used to enjoy, withdrawing from others, and being tired. People suffering from anxiety worry excessively and feel constantly stressed out. These signs are not as outwardly apparent as the aggressive or destructive behavior of those who have an oppositional defiant disorder or a conduct disorder, which is probably part of the reason why ADHD is more often diagnosed in boys than in girls.

Some of these comorbidities may develop as a consequence of the frustration and low self-esteem ADHD may have caused, which makes it all the more important that ADHD is identified as the root cause and treated properly.

are communicated in a way that people with ADHD can understand.

Studies have shown that a person with ADHD tends to forget instructions or goals if they are worded in an unspecific way. If they are specific, though, they are easier to remember and to follow. "Pick up your clothes and put them in the closet" is more likely to achieve the desired effect than the more general "clean your room." So-called "if-then" plans have proved to be effective in improving the self-control of people with ADHD. An if-then plan is a simple set of instructions consisting of a condition ("If you do x . . .") and a consequence (". . . then y happens."). This can take the form of a reward, which can help reinforce appropriate behavior ("If you do your homework within thew scheduled period of time, then you get a dollar.").

This technique can also be used by people to regulate their behavior by reining in impulsive reactions. A goal like "I want to be more attentive in school" is easier to reach when it is broken down into smaller, more specific steps, such as "If I feel my attention is

Talking to others who face the same difficulties and learning about their experiences can be rewarding and uplifting.

slipping, then I contribute to class to find my focus again."

Group therapy, which shows that you are not as alone with your problems as you may think you are, can be helpful as well. In mild cases of ADHD the behavioral approach is sometimes enough to resolve the issues.

The Pharmacological Approach

Pharmacological means of dealing with ADHD involve pharmaceuticals, which are drugs. The drugs most commonly used when treating ADHD are stimulants. Stimulants help you focus and get more work done. Many of these medications contain the active ingredient methylphenidate hydrochloride, which increases the activity of the neurotransmitters dopamine and noradrenaline. These are responsible for transmitting signals in the brain, particularly the parts of the brain controlling attention and behavior that are not as active in people with ADHD. The best-known of these drugs is Ritalin, but there are others (Equasym XL, Medikinet, Concerta XL) that contain the same active ingredient. A stimulant with different active ingredients is Adderall, which some people find has fewer side effects when the medication wears off compared to Ritalin.

Sometimes, a nonstimulant drug called atomoxetine, also known by the brand name Strattera, is used to treat ADHD. This is a norepinephrine reuptake inhibitor, which increases the concentration of that neurotransmitter in the brain and should have the same effect as a stimulant.

People react differently to medication, and it might take a doctor a while to figure out what works best and to find the optimal dose. This means that most likely the dosage will be adjusted frequently in the beginning. Especially in children and adolescents who are still growing, the dosage needs to be adjusted later on as well. If the treatment has been successful and the person taking the medication has been free of any ADHD symptoms for a long period of time, it might be a good idea to see if it is even needed anymore. You should

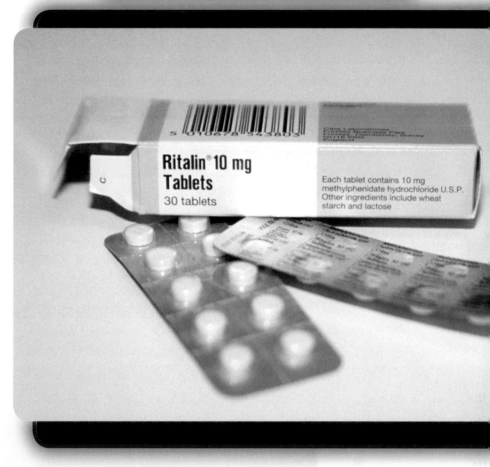

Ritalin® 10 mg Tablets
30 tablets

Each tablet contains 10 mg
methylphenidate hydrochloride U.S.P.
Other ingredients include wheat
starch and lactose

The right medication helps a lot of people with ADHD, but there is no universal remedy.

never stop taking your medication without consulting your doctor, though.

These drugs can have side effects, however, including headaches, stomachaches, decreased appetite, and difficulty sleeping. If you notice these or any other side effects, you should point them out to your doctor so that your treatment can be adjusted accordingly.

Some people are worried that taking ADHD medication will change a person's personality. Aside from the ability to concentrate better and being less impulsive, that should not be the case. Higher self-esteem can be a consequence of that, but that is hard to object to. If any changes beyond that become apparent, it should be pointed out to the doctor as the medication or the dosage may need to be changed.

Another common concern is that having to take drugs regularly from an early age could lead to problems with addiction later on, but this concern is unfounded. In fact, studies have shown that the risk for children with ADHD treated with stimulants tof developing a substance dependence is lower than for those not treated, as they have better control of their impulsivity.

On a general note, when dealing with drugs it is important to adhere to the doctor's orders. It should go without saying, but that includes not giving your medication to anybody else who may want to take it. And if you find that your doctor does not take your concerns and personal needs into consideration, it might be a good idea to get a second opinion.

The Multimodal Approach

The multimodal approach to dealing with ADHD involves more than one mode of addressing the symptoms, i.e., both behavioral therapy and medication. This combination is the most common form of treatment as it offers the most comprehensive approach. While medication can bring about great improvement quickly, it is not a miracle cure. It may make some things easier, but that does not mean everything will be easy. You still need to learn skills and develop habits to manage your condition, which often works best when supported by medication.

10 Great Questions to Ask a Health Care Professional

1. Do you have experience with ADHD?
2. How do you make a diagnosis?
3. How long will the evaluation take?
4. Can you rule out that these symptoms have a cause other than ADHD?
5. What kind of therapy do you suggest?
6. Do you think medication is necessary?
7. Which drugs do you recommend and how do they work?
8. What are possible side effects of the medication?
9. How do you propose to monitor and adjust the medication?
10. Could there be any coexisting conditions? How should those be addressed?

ADHD is most often associated with younger children because it is usually diagnosed at an early age. The symptom most apparent to the outside world, hyperactivity, tends to be less of an issue once a person with ADHD reaches their teens.

Other symptoms persist, though, and may even pose more difficulties than before as expectations and requirements increase. Puberty is a difficult time for everybody. Hormones are raging and your body is changing while you are trying to figure out who you are and who you want to be. School is becoming more demanding, both in regard to learning and navigating your social life. ADHD can make all that even more difficult.

As you get older, you are expected to manage a lot more assignments and activities and be more responsible, both in school and your family life, which many youths with ADHD struggle with. In some cases, these struggles lead to ADHD being diagnosed for the first time after it went unrecognized throughout childhood. Some particularly smart and talented individuals can compensate for the symptoms of ADHD for years without anybody recognizing them (although they may get to hear more often that they are not living up to their potential). But as their

Untreated, ADHD makes social interaction more difficult. As a consequence, those who have it are sometimes left out of the group.

responsibilities increase, they start to encounter problems, which may come as a shock.

It may be equally shocking for others who were diagnosed in childhood but were not able to fully comprehend their condition at the time. They may have been aware that they were somehow different from the other kids. But they are only beginning to truly realize what ADHD means for their lives once they reach their teenage years. The upside is that once you are old enough to understand the impact ADHD will have on your life, you are also old enough to get informed about the condition and the ways of managing it.

Being easily distracted is particularly dangerous when driving, so distractions should be kept to a minimum to lower the risk of an accident.

BEHIND THE WHEEL

Getting a license and being able to drive is a big step for many teenagers as it is a move toward independence. Not having to depend on your parents anymore to drive you and instead being able to go wherever you want whenever you want to is liberating, but with this freedom comes responsibility because there are potential dangers to consider.

It is prudent for every person operating a vehicle, but especially for new drivers, to minimize distractions as these can lead to accidents. Someone with ADHD who is easily distracted to begin with needs to be especially cautious. The impulsivity typical of many people with ADHD can also be a problem while driving. Studies have shown that young drivers with ADHD have a tendency toward risky driving behavior, are three times as likely to get a speeding

It is perfectly normal for adolescents going through puberty to test their boundaries to see how far they can go. For teenagers with ADHD, this can be dangerous because they often don't think about the consequences of their actions. If they have a tendency toward being rash and impulsive, they may take things too far and risk injury or other repercussions. This is especially true if they are being egged on by others.

Resisting peer pressure can be hard. For some youths with ADHD, risky behavior is a way to impress others, hoping it will make them popular. Some are "adrenaline junkies" who are constantly looking for a new thrill that can hold their interest for a while. Depending on the activity, that thrill may even lead to trouble with the law.

If you are looking for a way to defeat boredom, there are enough legal options available, such as martial arts or other sports. It is important to learn how to manage your impulses, to take a step back and think before you act. A therapist or coach can help you learn techniques to keep your impulses under control so that you won't get yourself into serious trouble.

Many teens experiment with alcohol, cigarettes, or drugs. The fact that these substances are forbidden may make them seem especially tempting, but they are forbidden for a reason. These substances can have a negative effect on your health, and using them can lead to addiction. The lack of impulse control in people with ADHD makes them more likely to overdo it and develop problems with substance abuse. Therefore it might be best to avoid situations in which you may be tempted. If you are having trouble with substance abuse, you should seek professional help.

ticket compared to their peers without ADHD, and are four times as likely to have an accident within the first two years after they get their license. But there are several things you can do to minimize the risk of causing harm to yourself or others.

It can help to get more practice operating a vehicle so that it requires less concentrated effort. Therefore it might be a good idea to drive with a responsible front seat passenger for a while even after you get your license or maybe even take some additional driver training classes. Plan your route beforehand. And if you should encounter an unforeseen obstacle (like the closure of a road) pull over and calmly adjust your plan. It is better to leave yourself plenty of time for your trip as you are more likely to make a mistake when you are in a rush.

Everything that could be a distraction should be avoided: turn off your cell phone; no eating or drinking; pick a music album or radio station beforehand and stick to it, or go without music entirely; only take your friends if they don't distract you, such as by talking too much. If possible, heavy traffic should be avoided, too.

You need to know your limits, and should that mean that you are not yet ready to drive even though you are old enough to have a license, it may be a tough choice to wait until you feel that you are ready, but it is the right decision.

Consult a doctor before changing medications to avoid unpleasant side effects.

TAKING MEDICATION

Once they reach their teenage years, people with ADHD often think about stopping their medication. They want to be in charge of their own lives, and discontinuing a drug you were told you have to take may seem like a good way to assert your independence.

You have to think about whether this is the right step, though. The purpose of the medication is to counterbalance a physical issue similar to glasses that are used to correct vision. Stopping medication would be like refusing to wear the glasses you need to see properly, and that would be a poor way to show your independence. It would only hinder yourself. Stopping medication, although it is helping you manage your symptoms, seems like cutting off your nose to spite your face. Doing what is best for your well-being shows far better that you can be independent.

If you feel that your medication is not helping you or that you don't need it anymore, talk about it with your doctor. He or she can adjust the dosage or monitor a test run without medication. It is unwise to try that without consulting a health care professional.

Some students with ADHD don't want to take their drugs in school because they fear they will be singled out. However, there is nothing shameful about taking medication that you need. While there are some drugs that need to be taken every few hours or so, there are alternatives that have to be taken only once a day so you can avoid having to take medicine in school.

CHAPTER 4

AROUND FAMILY AND FRIENDS

ADHD does not affect only the person who has it. Since the condition influences behavior, it is likely to also affect those the person interacts with, be it family, friends, or somebody encountered by chance. You are not at the mercy of your ADHD, though, and there are things you can do to make your relationships with others run more smoothly.

SPENDING TIME WITH FAMILY

You are around your family all the time, so your ADHD will likely have an effect on family life.

Parents of a young person with ADHD need to be informed

Getting the proper treatment for a child with ADHD can improve the quality of life for the whole family.

If all family members understand the difficulties of dealing with ADHD it can lead to a more harmonious family life.

about the disorder. While it has been established that bad parenting is not the cause of ADHD, that does not mean that parenting has no influence at all. How parents deal with their child has a great impact and can make living with ADHD better or worse.

Most parents want the best for their children, and they want to see them do well in school and succeed in life. If their child is inattentive, has a tendency to overreact, or has trouble in school it can be frustrating for the parents. It is important for them to understand that their child is not lazy or trying to hurt them on purpose, but that the things they find worrisome are symptoms of a medical condition that needs to be addressed. Rather than showing disappointment and reacting emotionally, parents need to help their child manage the symptoms

of the disorder by staying calm, being consistent, and using positive reinforcement and other strategies to make life together easier for everybody.

Structure and routine help individuals with ADHD control their symptoms, but it is natural for teenagers to object to the rules set by their parents. Some conflict is bound to occur. Parents should adjust their expectations. Expecting perfection is unreasonable, but expecting their child with ADHD to do the best they can is not. The same is true the other way around; parents are only human, too.

Parents need to act as advocates for their child and also teach the child to stand up for his or her own interests. Instead of simply deciding on their child's behalf, he or she—when old enough, which teenagers certainly are—should be actively involved in the decisions regarding treatment and dealing with the symptoms. ADHD is easiest to handle when the whole family is pulling together.

One thing to keep in mind is that ADHD is (at least partially) hereditary. If you have it, there's about a 40 percent chance that one of your parents has it, too. This can be a blessing and a curse. In the best case, it means that you have somebody who has gone through the same thing you are going through and can benefit from his or her experience. It can also mean that in arguments that arise between a parents and children, tempers are likely to flare, and shouting matches are a common occurrence. Since ADHD was not as well-known in their youth as it is now, many parents discover that they have it only after their child has been diagnosed with it. This knowledge can add

ADHD can hinder those that have it in developing social skills and have a negative impact on their social life. Individuals with ADHD, especially children, do not always notice how their behavior affects others. If they are impulsive, they may have a tendency to interrupt others or say things without thinking and filtering. Others may perceive this as rude, especially if they are not aware that a person with ADHD does not do this intentionally.

Some find it difficult to delay gratification, which others might see as being bossy and self-centered. Other common behaviors are reacting very strongly to a situation, being upset easily, and being aggressive toward others.

Inattentiveness can create the impression that people with ADHD are not interested in the conversation they are having or the person they are having it with. The tendency to forget things can lead others to believe that they cannot rely on the person with ADHD.

These skills can be worked on and improved. There are groups and training programs that focus on them. Role-playing exercises with a therapist can give you a better understanding of the impression your behavior creates and what you can do differently to leave a more positive impression. A family member can help you learn how to read body language and understand the subtext of a conversation, something many individuals with ADHD find difficult.

Social skills are acquired mainly through watching and copying the behavior of other people, so the best way to hone them is to get out there and practice.

ADD/ADHD AND SOCIAL SKILLS

It isn't always easy for the siblings of a child with ADHD to deal with the situation.

to the difficulties, but it can also be an important step toward making the family's situation more manageable.

Siblings are affected by ADHD as well. About 25 percent of the brothers and sisters of someone with ADHD have it, too. But even if they don't have it, it has an effect on them. For siblings, especially when they are younger, it is often hard to understand why their brother or sister is getting more attention, even if the attention is the result of a medical condition. And sometimes they feel like victims of their brother or sister's behavior, either directly (particularly if the sibling with ADHD also has ODD or CD and has a tendency to be aggressive) or indirectly (when fun activities or events have to be cut short or cancelled out of consideration for their sibling's ADHD). This can put additional stress on the family. There is no easy solution. The whole family has to work together. Everybody has to make sacrifices and try to make the best of the situation.

Every teenager will argue with their parents about the rules they set and the chores they expect to be done. For teenagers with ADHD, it can be helpful to have the reasons behind those rules laid out. Parents don't usually set rules just to be mean, although their children may get that impression sometimes. It is

a good idea to talk about why the rules are necessary and maybe negotiate a situation that works for everybody.

It can also be helpful to have the rules in writing and keep the list somewhere visible so that it can function as a reminder. The same works well for chores. It can be extremely annoying to have a chore sprung on you. Having a reminder list makes chores more manageable. It is also satisfying when you can cross off something you have done.

Chores are not only a way to help out your parents and contribute. They are also important life lessons that you need to learn. Eventually you will have to be able to get your grocery shopping done, clean your house, wash your clothes, and many other things. When you go off to college or move into your own place, there will be nobody there to do it for you, so it will be valuable to know how to do these things.

HANGING OUT WITH FRIENDS

Some people with ADHD are very popular because others appreciate their enthusiastic, energetic nature or their creative side. But there are also many who find it difficult to make friends and to maintain friendships, sometimes up to the point where they feel rejected and socially isolated. ADHD can make it difficult to develop social

Friends come and go. Family can often be relied upon when you can't turn to others.

skills during childhood. As a result, many individuals with ADHD have trouble with social interactions into adulthood. This can be especially painful during your teenage years, as friends offer an important port of call away from your parents.

Having ADHD does not mean that you are doomed to be a social outcast. Social skills can be practiced. School clubs or other group activities are a great opportunity to practice them. If you are interested in the activity, you will find it easier to focus. And since the others taking part are interested in the same thing as you, you will find it easier to interact with them as you automatically have something to talk about.

Athletic activities are great for people with ADHD. Research indicates that exercise has a positive effect on attention problems. Aside from the physical activity, many sports also focus on practicing self-control, which can be particularly valuable for an individual with ADHD, and they can be good for your self-esteem.

When in a conversation, do your best to listen and not interrupt. Simply taking a deep breath before you say something can be enough to stop yourself from speaking without thinking and blurting out something that might hurt the other person. Ask questions to keep the conversation going. Not only will it help you stay focused, it will also show the person you are talking with that you are interested.

Frequent eye contact will help with that as well. People like it when you show an interest in them. It makes them feel important and maybe a little flattered. As a result, they will be more likely to show an interest in you as well.

Consider telling your friends about your ADHD. You may be embarrassed, but knowing about ADHD and its symptoms will help them understand your behavior. If they know the reason why you are inattentive, impulsive, or forgetful at times, they are likely to be more understanding. And if someone rejects you because of your ADHD, that person was not much of a friend to begin with. You are better off finding this out sooner rather than later.

THE DATING LIFE

Dating presents teens with ADHD with the same problems as friendship, but to a higher degree. A first date can be particularly stressful and exciting. The same social skills apply to dating as a conversation with a friend, but you should be extra careful. When romantic feelings are involved, it is easier for a person to be hurt or disappointed.

You may want to prepare some questions beforehand if you fear you might not be able to think of something on the spot so you can show interest in your date and prevent your conversation from coming to a halt. If you think your excitement may lead you to talk too much, come up with a signal that will remind you to stop. Consider if a group date is an option. It can take some of the pressure off. If you have trouble understanding

Dating is an exciting part of teenage life, but there are some pitfalls to avoid when ADHD is involved.

the nonverbal cues involved in flirting and dating, try to learn about them. Watching romantic movies can help with that. If you are unsure about the signals he or she is sending, ask your date. This may be a little embarrassing, but it could save you from the much bigger embarrassment of misreading them entirely.

You don't need to bring up your ADHD on the first date, but once you have been dating someone for a while, you should talk about the disorder and how its symptoms could affect the relationship. If you should forget a date because of your ADHD, your partner will probably be more understanding if he or she knows the reason and doesn't think you are simply inconsiderate.

Difficulties with impulse control and a lack of forethought are reasons why teens with ADHD are at a greater risk to catch a sexually transmitted disease and to be involved in an unwanted pregnancy. Some girls who suffer from low self-esteem as a consequence of their ADHD are promiscuous in the hopes of making themselves more popular. Talk about sex with your parents or a counselor, inform yourself about safe sex and contraception, and if you decide to become sexually active, be sure that it is not for the wrong reasons.

5

School is problematic for many people with ADHD. In fact, the condition is often first discovered after a young person has started going to school because the demands of the new situation make the disorder apparent. These include being expected to sit still for extended amounts of time and to learn about things they aren't necessarily interested in. And the demands of school only grow, especially once you reach middle and high school. Students are expected to take more responsibility for their school work. Students with ADHD often struggle with this. As a result, young people with ADHD are three times as likely as their peers without the disorder to have to repeat a year at least once. Also, roughly a third leave school without graduating. But there are methods that can help you master the challenges and be successful in school.

TALKING WITH TEACHERS

If 5 to 8 percent of all children have ADHD, that means there is an average of one in every class. Most teachers are aware of the condition, but there is no guarantee that they are experts in regard to ADHD or that they know how to react to a student who has it. They may not recognize

Many teachers are happy to support their students in overcoming their difficulties. Talking with them about ADHD is a good way to help them help you.

that inattentiveness, a lack of concentration, impulsive behavior, and difficulties with assignments are symptoms of ADHD. If they attribute these behaviors to causes other than ADHD, it is possible that they could react to them in a way that is counterproductive. While disciplinary measures may have the desired effect in other cases, they won't make the symptoms of ADHD go away. Instead they are likely to make the student resent the teacher, making it less likely that they will follow the class with interest.

You may be reluctant to let your teachers know about your condition, but it

Your Rights in School

In the United States, there are two important federal laws that can have an impact on the education of a student with ADHD. The Individuals with Disabilities Education Act (IDEA) is an educational benefit law that offers additional services to those who need them. Section 504 of the Rehabilitation Act of 1973 is a civil rights law meant to ensure that individuals with disabilities have the same access to a public education as others. Both of these laws have the same goal. The requirements to be eligible for IDEA are stricter. Section 504 uses a broader definition of what a disability is. This means that students with ADHD are covered more often under Section 504 than under IDEA. A prerequisite for both is an official evaluation.

If a student is found to be in need of special education, IDEA ensures that he or she is provided with an Individualized Education Program (IEP) developed by a team consisting of school staff, the parents of the student, and the student themselves. This program is tailored to the student's individual needs and can entail individual instruction by specialists as well as accommodations like extra time for assignments or tests. Annual goals are set and the program is reviewed at least once a year to make sure the student gets the help he or she needs.

Students who qualify under Section 504 will receive an educational plan as well, and they are entitled to certain modifications and accommodations, like preferential seating or extended time.

The purpose of these laws is to help those who meet the requirements to achieve their full potential in school and level the playing field. There is no shame in that, and if you are having trouble in school because of ADHD, you should look into the options that are open to you.

can help make things easier for both sides. For someone to offer you the help you need, they first have to be aware that you need it. A good teacher will be willing to learn about ADHD and employ methods that will assist their student in succeeding in class. This could include keeping instructions clear and concise, writing assignments on the board rather than just saying what they want you to do, outlining their expectations in a detailed manner, and being patient, even if you have to ask about something several times before you can remember. Depending on how much the disorder affects your ability to learn, you may be legally entitled to certain accommodations to help you study better.

If you are worried that your teacher might embarrass you in front of the class, ask him to talk with you in private about anything that has to do with your ADHD. There can be an upside to classmates knowing about it. They may be more understanding than you expect. However, it should be your decision whom you tell or don't tell about it.

WORKING IN SCHOOL

There are some ways to help you get organized and stay focused in school. First, you need to make sure that you bring everything you need with you. Keep a list near the door of your house so you can check and double-check before you leave home.

If possible, choose a place to sit that keeps you from getting distracted. That could mean sitting up front near

If you tend to forget things, the best thing you can do is take notes that are as clear and specific as possible.

the teacher, where the conversations of your peers are less likely to draw away your focus from the lesson, and/or sitting with your back turned to the window. Sitting by yourself cuts down on distractions, but sometimes having a calm and quiet neighbor can have a positive effect.

Only put things on your desk that you actually need for class, and avoid clutter. Use a different color notebook and matching folder for every subject. That way you can easily recognize where to take down your notes for every class.

Keep track of upcoming tests and long-term assignments with a day planner or calendar so they won't be forgotten and you can prepare for them. You could use a smartphone or tablet for this, but a printed version has the advantage that you don't need to worry about power supply.

Find a way of taking notes that works for you, whether that means writing down everything the teacher says or only the main ideas, focusing on how the information could be applied to the real world, or translating it into charts or mind maps. The important thing is that you can find the key information quickly and easily.

Leave enough space so that you can add information later. Add a question mark to remind you to ask your teacher if there is something you did not understand. Going over your notes again within twenty-four hours will help you absorb the material and store it in your long-term memory. Reviewing them with the teacher or a classmate is a good opportunity to resolve any issues. If you have trouble listening and taking notes at the same time, see if you can get notes from a friend or the teacher and make sure you understand them.

Having a reliable, well-organized study partner can be a great help. But you need to make sure your partner gets something out of the cooperation as well. Find somebody who can benefit from your strengths just as you benefit from his or hers.

Use self-monitoring to track how much you were paying attention in class. Also, record the reasons why you might have been distracted so that you can avoid those in the future. To do this, prepare a chart for each period. Every few minutes make a short note to indicate whether you were paying attention or not. A plus sign and a minus sign will suffice. The chart should not itself become a distraction, of course. This technique can be useful outside of school as well, be it for homework or other activities.

Doing Homework

To be able to do your homework assignments, you first need to know what they are. It is essential to keep a notebook in which you write down your assignments for the day and when you need them to be done. The more detailed your notes, the less likely it is for there to be misunderstandings. For example, rather than simply writing down "math problems," it is better to be specific: "math problems, #4–7, p. 64." This leaves no room for error.

If there is no assignment for a class it is important to make a note of that, too. Don't just leave a blank space, which might lead to confusion. Simply writing down "no assignment" makes clear that you did not forget.

If you have trouble remembering taking your notes, you could ask the teacher or a reliable classmate to check or sign off on them to ensure that you have all the information you need. Or maybe your teachers are willing to e-mail you the assignments. And if for some reason you

Developing a routine for studying can help you keep focus. You just need to find out what works best for you.

do forget something, you need to know whom you can ask to get the information you need.

To help structure your work, it is beneficial to have both a time and a place set aside for homework assignments. Some prefer to tackle their homework as soon as they get out of school. What they learned is still fresh in their minds and they may want to have it out of the way as quickly as possible. Others prefer to take a break and do something else first. You have to see what works best for you and stick to that time to develop a routine. Generally it is not a good idea to wait

Using a timer when doing schoolwork is a good way to focus and stay on track.

until the last possible moment, though, as the added pressure can lead to frustration.

The place where you do your homework, preferably a desk, should have all the things on hand that you need for your assignments. Every time you need to get up to get something, there is a chance you will get distracted.

If possible, keep an extra set of textbooks at home as well. If you can't reserve a spot solely for the purpose of doing your homework, you can keep all the things you need in a box that you pull out when it is time

Both at home and at school, a well-organized work area can be a great help to keep focus and not let yourself be distracted.

to get to work. This way turning the kitchen table (or whichever spot you choose) into your work area takes only a second.

Your homework location should be well-lit and quiet. Television and music serve as distractions and should be avoided. Also, it should be free from clutter.

Before you start, take a look at your assignments and make sure that you understand what you need to do. Read any questions or details of a problem carefully. Break down your tasks into steps to make them more manageable if necessary.

Then decide in which order to work on your assignments. Usually it is best to start with the most difficult assignment or the subject you dislike the most rather than have it looming at the end. This way you are not in danger of dragging out your other assignments to avoid it. You can also reward yourself with an easier task after the worst is out of the way.

Write down everything you need to do in the form of a list where you can cross off completed tasks as you work through them. This is especially helpful for long-term projects. Make a note of how long you expect a task will take you, keep track of how long it actually takes you, and compare the two. If you have a tendency to be overly optimistic with your estimates, this will improve the accuracy of your planning.

Taking a short break of about five minutes every half hour or so can be great for recharging your batteries. If you find yourself not returning to your work after your break is over, set a timer that will call you back to your desk.

Once you are done, be sure to pack your homework in your school bag. It would be a shame to have gone through all the trouble and then not be able to present your results. Having a designated folder for completed homework assignments can help you not to forget.

Putting a routine in place can be difficult at first, but if you stick to it there should be positive results soon. If you continue to have trouble with your homework despite your best effort to approach it in a well-structured manner, it might be worth considering if there is a reason for it other than an attention deficit. Not everybody is good at everything, and even the best work ethics will only help so much if you are having trouble with the subject matter. It could be that a tutor is needed.

TACKLING TESTS

Tests are a way for students to demonstrate how much they have learned and how well they understand the material. Many students with ADHD dread them. But good preparation can make taking tests a lot less stressful.

If you are keeping track of upcoming tests in your calendar, they won't come as a surprise, and you will have enough time to study. Cramming the night before the test is usually a recipe for disaster. There is a good chance you won't be able to remember what you learned. Spreading out your learning sessions over several days will not only help you retain the information but it will also give you the opportunity to ask about anything you may have found unclear while going through your notes. Check with your teacher what information the test will cover, where the focus will lie, and what format the test will take (true-false questions, multiple choice, essay, etc.).

Make sure that you have all the information you need to prepare. If you find that you have trouble

remembering things you learned, look into memorization techniques, like using flash cards or developing a story that links the items to remember, and find one that works for you.

Once the test starts, read the directions at least two times, and make sure that you understand what you need to do. Write down quick notes about information you think is important but fear you might forget while working on the test. This way you have it available when you need it. Finally, check your work carefully before turning it in.

If your test scores do not improve despite your best efforts to study, you should see if there are any accommodations (like being allowed extra time) open to you.

Many students with ADHD dread tests they have to take. But with the right preparation, the stress can be reduced considerably.

6

MOVING FORWARD

For a long time it was believed that ADHD stopped being an issue once an individual diagnosed with it reached adulthood, but sadly that is not the case. Studies show that about 60 percent still struggle with attention problems, impulsivity, and inner restlessness. As a result, adults with ADHD are less likely to graduate from college and tend to have trouble getting organized and managing their day-to-day responsibilities. They are also likely to encounter problems in their relationships and change jobs more frequently. This in turn can lead to

Although many students with ADHD struggle in school, it is possible to succeed despite the difficulties the disorder causes.

a strong sense of underachievement, frustration, and low self-esteem. The earlier you understand the challenges of living with ADHD and learn the necessary skills to keep your symptoms under control, the better off you will be.

Life After High School

It's a big decision for everybody if they want to go to college or not, probably even more so for somebody with ADHD. School is difficult for many students with ADHD, and when they are done, it does not seem appealing to them to continue studying. As a result, only about one out of five high school students with ADHD goes on to attend college.

In school you are forced to study many subjects you may not be interested in. This makes paying attention difficult. In college on the other hand, you can choose your own courses and pick classes that are appealing to you, so that may not be as much of an issue.

College life will give you a lot more independence and personal freedom, which can be a double-edged sword. There is less supervision and less structure. You need to be sure that you can manage your classes, long-term assignments, and your chores without parents and teachers providing a routine for you. Adapting to this can be difficult even for those who do not have ADHD. There are many temptations that can draw you away from your work. Nobody will remind you to eat healthy and regularly, to get enough sleep, to get up in time for class, or to take your medication. You have to be self-sufficient. The earlier you start honing the skills you will need, the better.

Colleges are legally required to offer reasonable accommodations for students with ADHD (help with taking notes, extra time on exams). However, you have to make the school aware of how the disorder impairs your ability to learn to get the assistance you need. This should be done at the earliest possible opportunity. Once you run into trouble because of your ADHD, it may be too late. It is a good idea to get in contact with the office of disability support services of the colleges you consider before you even apply to find out what kind of support the schools offer. These services differ, which may influence your decision for or against a school. They will also be able to tell you if there is a student support group for ADHD on campus.

Applying for colleges is in itself a scary task. Filling out application forms, writing essays, and asking for letters of recommendation can be overwhelming. But getting support from your parents or a specialized coach or tutor will make it more manageable.

Going to college is not your only option after graduating from high school. A community college may be a good way to test the waters of higher education without moving (far) away from home. Community colleges offer two-year associate degrees

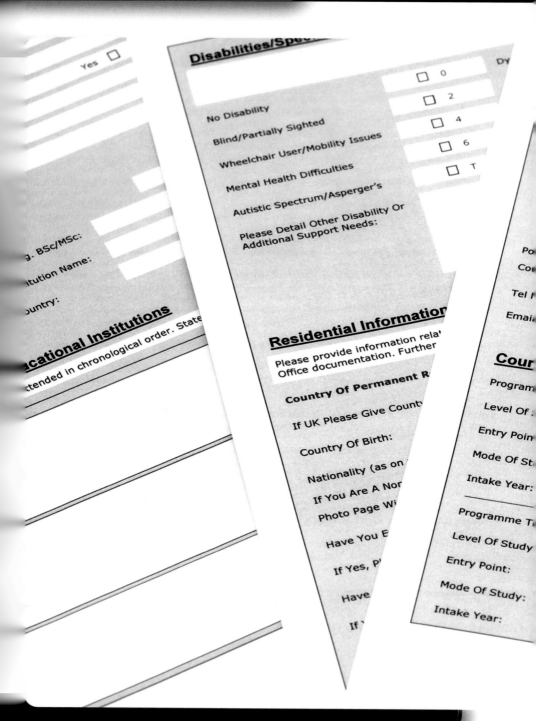

Yes ☐

g. BSc/MSc:
itution Name:
ountry:

cational Institutions

tended in chronological order. State

Disabilities/Spe

☐ 0
☐ 2
☐ 4
☐ 6
☐ T

No Disability

Blind/Partially Sighted

Wheelchair User/Mobility Issues

Mental Health Difficulties

Autistic Spectrum/Asperger's

Please Detail Other Disability Or
Additional Support Needs:

DY

Residential Information

Please provide information rela
Office documentation. Further

Country Of Permanent R

If UK Please Give Count

Country Of Birth:

Nationality (as on

If You Are A Nor
Photo Page Wi

Have You E

If Yes, P

Have

If

Po
Co

Tel
Emai

Cour

Program
Level Of
Entry Poin
Mode Of St
Intake Year:

Programme T
Level Of Study
Entry Point:
Mode Of Study:
Intake Year:

Regional ID/ Agent Code:

Full Time Undergraduate applications should be submi   This form is to

Personal Details

Family Name:

Previous Name:

Date Of Birth: (DD/MM/YY)

Permanent Address:

e:

s) Applied For

Title:

Undergraduate ☐

Year 1   ☐

Full Time ☐   Year

                Part Time ☐

Undergraduate ☐

Year 1   ☐

Full Time ☐   Ye

            Part Time ☐

Completing college applications may seem daunting to someone with ADHD, but the payoffs of a college education are well worth the effort.

that can qualify you for many different jobs (such as a technician, registered nurse, paralegal, web developer, or construction manager). Community colleges tend to focus more on hands-on experience than four-year colleges do, which makes it easier for many people with ADHD to learn. If you want to continue your studies, you can transfer to a university after graduating from community college to pursue a bachelor's degree.

Vocational schools or trade schools prepare for specific, typically blue-collar jobs (such as a

FINDING THE RIGHT JOB

Career satisfaction is important for everybody, but for individuals with ADHD it is crucial. Without satisfaction in their work, they are more likely to get fired or change jobs frequently. Finding a job that you are passionate about will help you stay focused, be motivated, and consequently be more successful.

There is no definite list of careers that are particularly well suited to people with ADHD, as it depends on the individual's interests, strengths, and weaknesses. If you are having trouble sitting still, it is obviously not prudent to choose a career that requires you to work at a desk all day. But there are opportunities that play to the strengths of people with ADHD.

Working as a salesperson gives you the opportunity to act with many different people. Also, the enthusiasm characteristic of many people with ADHD can be a great plus. Being creative and highly energetic are good qualifications for working as an artist or an entertainer. Being self-employed can be a good option, as it allows the opportunity to take on many different projects while making your own schedule. You also need to be open to taking some risks, which people without ADHD generally have more of a problem with.

The high-intensity environment of a hospital may be the right thing for you, be it as a nurse or as a doctor. Getting a medical degree is hard work, but ADHD will not prevent you from reaching a goal you are truly passionate about. The ability to hyperfocus can work to your benefit if you find the job that is right for you.

carpenter, jeweler, or auto mechanic). These are usually very hands-on.

Some young people decide to join the work force right away. This can work out well if they find a job they enjoy and are qualified for. By working part-time during high school, some students with ADHD find a job they are passionate about.

MINDING YOUR MONEY

Time management and impulse control are difficult for many people with ADHD, and as a result they may have a tendency to splurge. That is usually not a big problem as long as you are living at home and your basic needs like food and shelter are covered. Even if you spend your allowance on the first day of the month, there is no lasting harm done, although you may have some long weeks ahead of you.

The repercussions of not being responsible with your money are of course far more severe once you have your own income and need to pay your own bills. Then thinking about whether you can actually afford something rather than buying things on a whim can make the difference between having to go hungry or not.

Being good with money is a skill that can and should be learned. Start practicing with a weekly budget, then a biweekly budget, then a monthly budget. When saving up for something, set yourself a very specific goal and write

Being able to manage your money is an important life skill, especially if you have a tendency to be impulsive.

it down. For example, when saving for a video game, take down the name and the amount it is going to cost and keep that note somewhere visible so it can work as a reminder.

Opening a checking account and/or getting a charge card with a very low limit while still in high school can be a good learning experience. If you think you can handle it and your parents are up to it, being put in charge of a larger sum as a test run will give you the chance to show that you can live within your means. It's better to fail in such a controlled environment than later on in life when going into debt can have ruinous repercussions. Hopefully such an experience would be a valuable lesson.

If you find that you have constant problems organizing your finances, it might be a good idea to seek help when planning your budget, be it from a parent, a trusted friend, or a professional.

GLOSSARY

ADD (attention deficit disorder) An older term for ADHD, often used interchangeably, sometimes used to describe the predominantly inattentive representation of ADHD.

ADHD (attention-deficit/hyperactivity disorder) A behavioral disorder characterized by inattention, impulsivity, and hyperactivity.

coexisting condition Conditions a person has in addition to another. For example, conduct disorder is a common coexisting condition in children with ADHD.

combined representation One of the three subtypes of ADHD described in the *DSM*. It combines the symptoms of the other two subtypes, the predominantly hyperactive-impulsive and the predominantly inattentive representation.

conduct disorder A psychological disorder diagnosed in childhood and adolescence characterized by difficulties following rules as well as aggressive behavior.

DSM (Diagnostic and Statistical Manual of Mental Disorders) This is the standard classification published by the American Psychiatric Association.

hyperactivity Abnormal activity, such as not being able to sit still and running around all the time.

hyperfocus A focus on something to the point that you are oblivious to your surroundings and lose track of time.

hyperkinetic disorder The name for ADHD used in the *International Classification of Diseases*, the standard diagnostic tool published by the World Health Organization.

IDEA (Individuals with Disabilities Education Act) An educational benefit law ensuring that those who need it will get special education, for which some individuals with ADHD are eligible.

IEP (individualized education plan) A plan tailored to the needs of a student meeting the requirements for special education under the Individuals with Disabilities Education Act.

impulsivity Being rash; acting or reacting before thinking.

multimodal treatment A treatment using different disciplines; in the case of ADHD, a treatment that relies on medication and therapy.

neurotransmitter A chemical that transmits signals from one brain cell to another.

predominantly hyperactive-impulsive representation One of the three subtypes of ADHD described in the *DSM*, characterized by the symptoms of hyperactivity and impulsivity.

predominantly inattentive representation One of the three subtypes of ADHD described in the DSM, characterized by the symptom of inattentiveness.

Ritalin A stimulant commonly used to treat the symptoms of ADHD.

Section 504 A section of the Rehabilitation Act of 1973, a civil rights law that prohibits discrimination against individuals with disabilities, affording students with ADHD certain accommodations in school.

stimulant A drug that temporarily increases alertness and attention. Stimulants such as Ritalin or Adderall are often used to treat the symptoms of ADHD.

Strattera A nonstimulant medication used to treat the symptoms of ADHD.

FOR MORE INFORMATION

ADDitude magazine
39 West 37th Street, 15th Floor
New York, NY 10018
Website: http://www.additudemag.com
ADDitude magazine, founded in 1998, offers practical
 information for individuals of all ages affected by
 ADHD, including tips for organization and education. Its website also features an active community
 called ADDConnect.

Canadian Attention Deficit Hyperactivity Disorder
 Resource Alliance (CADDRA)
3950 14th Avenue, Suite 604
Markham, ON L3R 0A9
Canada
(416) 637-8583
Website: http://www.caddra.ca
The Canadian Attention Deficit Hyperactivity
 Disorder Resource Alliance is a nonprofit alliance
 of Canadian health care professionals aiming to
 improve the life of patients with ADHD and their
 families.

Centre for ADHD Awareness Canada (CADDAC)
3950 14th Avenue, Suite 604
Markham, ON L3R 0A9

Canada

(416) 637-8584

Website: http://www.caddac.ca

This is a nonprofit organization providing advocacy
for individuals with ADHD across Canada in areas
such as education, health, and employment.

Children and Adults with Attention-Deficit/
Hyperactivity Disorder (CHADD)

4601 Presidents Drive, Suite 300

Lanham, MD 20706

(301) 306-7070

Website: http://www.chadd.org

This nonprofit organization with more than twelve
thousand members provides education, advocacy,
and support for individuals with ADHD. In
addition to its website and printed materials,
it also offers training and events for parents,
teachers, and professionals.

National Center on Birth Defects and Developmental
Disabilities (NCBDDD)

Division of Human Development and Disabilities

Mail-Stop E87

1600 Clifton Road

Atlanta, GA 30333

(800) 232-4636

Website: http://www.cdc.gov/ncbddd/adhd

Part of the Centers for Disease Control and

Prevention, the NCBDDD's mission is to identify the causes of developmental disabilities and to help children reach their full potential. In addition to scientific articles and statistics, its website features free materials like a symptoms checklist and informative posters.

National Institute of Mental Health
Science Writing, Press, and Dissemination Branch
6001 Executive Boulevard, Room 6200, MSC 9663
Bethesda, MD 20892-9663
(866) 615-6464
Website: http://www.nlm.nih.gov/medlineplus/attentiondeficithyperactivitydisorder.html
The National Institute of Mental Health is part of the U.S. Department of Health and Human Services and its mission is to transform the understanding and treatment of mental illnesses. Its website offers a lot of information on ADHD and related issues.

National Resource Center on ADHD
CHADD
4601 Presidents Drive, Suite 300
Lanham, MD 20706
(800) 233-4050
Website: http://www.help4adhd.org
A program of CHADD established in 2002, the NRC aims to raise public awareness about ADHD and improve the health and quality of

life of people affected by ADHD by expanding their knowledge of the issues related to the disorder. To this end, its information specialists respond to questions related to ADHD via telephone or its website.

WEBSITES

Because of the changing nature of Internet links, Rosen Publishing has developed an online list of websites related to the subject of this book. This site is updated regularly. Please use this link to access the list:

http://www.rosenlinks.com/411/ADD

FOR FURTHER READING

Ashley, Susan. *1000 Best Tips for ADHD: Expert Answers and Bright Advice to Help You and Your Child*. Naperville, IL: Sourcebooks, 2012.

Barkley, Russell A. *Taking Charge of ADHD: The Complete, Authoritative Guide for Parents*. New York, NY: The Guilford Press, 2013.

Brown, Richard P., and Patricia L. Gerbarg. *Non-Drug Treatments for ADHD: New Options for Kids, Adults, and Clinicians*. New York, NY: W. W. Norton & Company, 2012.

Brown, Thomas E. *Smart but Stuck: Emotions in Teens and Adults with ADHD*. San Francisco, CA: Jossey-Bass, 2014.

Dendy, Chris A. Zeigler. *Teaching Teens with ADD, ADHD & Executive Function Deficits: A Quick Reference Guide for Teachers and Parents*. 2nd ed. Bethesda, MD: Woodbine House, 2011.

Denevi, Timothy. *Hyper: A Personal History of ADHD*. New York, NY: Simon & Schuster, 2014.

Forgan, James W., and Mary Anne Richey. *Raising Boys with ADHD: Secrets for Parenting Healthy, Happy Sons*. Waco, TX: Prufrock Press, 2012.

Forgan, James W., and Mary Anne Richey. *Raising Girls with ADHD: Secrets for Parenting Healthy, Happy Daughters*. Waco, TX: Prufrock Press, 2014.

Gillberg, Christopher. *ADHD and Its Many Associated Problems*. Oxford, England: Oxford University Press, 2014.

Hawthorne, Susan. *Accidental Intolerance: How We Stigmatize ADHD and How We Can Stop*. Oxford, England: Oxford University Press, 2014.

Hinshaw, Stephen P. *The ADHD Explosion: Myths, Medication, Money, and Today's Push for Performance*. New York, NY: Oxford University Press, 2014.

Honos-Webb, Lara. *The ADHD Workbook for Teens: Activities to Help You Gain Motivation and Confidence*. Oakland, CA: Instant Help Books, 2010.

Levrini, Abigail, and Frances Prevatt. *Succeeding with Adult ADHD: Daily Strategies to Help You Achieve Your Goals and Manage Your Life*. Washington, DC: American Psychological Association, 2012.

Quinn, Patricia O. *AD/HD and the College Student: The Everything Guide to Your Most Urgent Questions*. Washington, DC: Magination Press, 2012.

Quinn, Patricia O. *100 Questions & Answers About Attention-Deficit Hyperactivity Disorder (AD/HD) in Women and Girls*. Sudburry, MA: Jones & Bartlett Learning, 2011.

Quinn, Patricia O. *On Your Own: A College Readiness Guide for Teens with ADHD/LD*. Washington, DC: Magination Press, 2011.

Quinn, Patricia O. *Putting on the Brakes: Understanding and Taking Control of Your ADD or ADHD*. 3rd ed. Washington, DC: Magination Press, 2012.

Spodak, Ruth. *Take Control of ADHD: The Ultimate Guide for Teens with Attention Problems*. Waco, TX: Prufrock Press, 2011.

Tournemille, Harry. *Attention Deficit Hyperactivity Disorder*. New York, NY: Crabtree Publishing Company, 2014.

Weyandt, Lisa L. *College Students with ADHD: Current Issues and Future Directions*. New York, NY: Springer, 2013.

Yarney, Susan. *Can I Tell You About ADHD? A Guide for Friends, Family and Professionals*. London, England: Jessica Kingsley Publishers, 2013.

BIBLIOGRAPHY

Alexander-Roberts, Colleen. *ADHD and Teens: A Parent's Guide to Making It Through the Tough Years*. Dallas, TX: Taylor Publishing, 1995.

Barkley, Russell A. *Das große ADHS-Handbuch für Eltern: Verantwortung übernehmen für Kinder mit Aufmerksamkeitsdefizit und Hyperaktivität*. 3rd ed. Bern, Switzerland: Verlang Hans Huber, 2011.

Buningh, Susan, Terry Illes, and Rob Tudisco. "Disclosure in Educational Settings." Chadd.org, April 2009. Retrieved October 2, 2014 (http://www.chadd.org/Portals/0/AM/Images/Understading/APRIL09_ATE_Illes_and_Tudisco.pdf).

Children and Adults with Attention-Deficit/Hyperactivity Disorder. "The Disorder Named ADHD." 2004. Retrieved September 24, 2014 (http://www.help4adhd.org/documents/wwk1.pdf).

Döpfner, Manfred, Jan Frölich, and Tanja Wolff Metternich. *Ratgeber ADHS: Informationen für Betroffene, Eltern, Lehrer und Erzieher zu Aufmerksamkeitsdefizit-/Hyperaktivitätsstörungen*. 2nd ed. Göttingen, Germany: Hofgrefe Verlag, 2007.

Friedman, Grace. "Embracing Your ADHD. A Free Guide for Teens with ADHD." Addyteen.com. Retrieved October 8, 2014 (http://www.addyteen.com/adhd/system/files/EmbracingYourADHD_1.pdf

?file=1&type=node&id=71&destination=node/71).

Gawrilow, Caterina, Peter M. Gollwitzer, and Gabriele Oettingen. "If-Then Plans Benefit Delay of Gratification Performance in Children With and Without ADHD." Springer Science+Business Media, May 1, 2010. Retrieved October 8, 2014 (http://www.psych.nyu.edu/gollwitzer/Gawrilow%20 Gollwitzer%20Oettingen_Delay%20Paper_ CoTR_2011-1.pdf).

Gawrilow, Caterina. *Lehrbuch ADHS*. Munich, Germany: Ernst Reinhardt Verlag, 2012

Krowatschek, Dieter. *Alles über ADS: Ein Ratgeber für Eltern*. 4th ed. Düsseldorf, Germany: Patmos Verlag, 2003.

Lange, Klaus W., et al. "The History of Attention Deficit Hyperactivity Disorder." Springer Open Choice, November 30, 2010. Retrieved October 7, 2014 (http://www.ncbi.nlm.nih.gov/pmc/articles/ PMC3000907/).

Mähler, Bettina, and Martin Schmela. *Albtraum ADS: Wie Eltern sich helfen können*. Reinbek bei Hamburg, Germany: Rowohlt Taschenbuch Verlag, 2007.

Nadeau, Kathleen. "High School Girls with AD/ HD." Chadd.org, November 2000. Retrieved October 2, 2014 (http://www.chadd. org/Portals/0/AM/Images/Understading/ NOV2000HighSchoolGirlsWithADHD.pdf).

Neuhaus, Cordula. *Jugendliche mit AD(H)S: Wie Erwachsenwerden gelingt*. Rev. ed. Freiburg, Germany: Urania Verlag, 2009.

Pomeroy, Ross. "The False ADHD Controversy." *Real Clear Science*, December 15, 2013. Retrieved October 7, 2014 (http://www.realclearscience.com/blog/2013/12/should_we_stop_treating_adhd.html/).

Rabiner, David. "The Impact of ADHD on Siblings." Helpforadd.com, 2006. Retrieved October 16, 2014 (http://www.helpforadd.com/add-impact-on-siblings/).

Robin, Arthur L. *ADHD in Adolescents: Diagnosis and Treatment*. New York, NY: Guilford Press, 1998.

Schleider, Karin. *ADHS: Wissen was stimmt*. Freiburg im Breisgau, Germany: Herder Verlag, 2009.

Tanner, T. Bradley, and Mary P. Metcalf. "ADHD Success Guide for Teens." Clinical Tools, Inc., February 2001. Retrieved October 8, 2004 (http://www.adhd.co.il/pdf/teenGuideFinal.pdf).

U.S. Department of Education. "Identifying and Treating Attention Deficit Hyperactivity Disorder. A Resource for School and Home." 2003. Retrieved September 14, 2014 (http://www2.ed.gov/teachers/needs/speced/adhd/adhd-resource-pt1.pdf).

Weiss, Lynn. *Leben mit ADS*. Moers, Germany: Joh. Brendow & Sohn Verlag, 2003.

INDEX

A

Adderall, 36
addiction, 38, 46
adulthood
  dealing with ADHD as an
    adult, 84, 86
alcohol, 46
  use during pregnancy, 12
anxiety disorder, 32
attention-deficit disorder, 7,
  14, 18
attention-deficit/
  hyperactivity disorder
  (ADHD)
  causes, 11–13, 17
  diagnosing, 17, 24, 26–27,
    32, 40, 43
  history of, 16, 18–19,
    21–22
  and intelligence, 9, 29
  misdiagnoses, 29
  myths and facts about, 23
  questions as to its
    existence, 17
  strengths of those with,
    9, 11
  symptoms of, 4, 7
  tests for, 17
  treatment, 27, 31, 33,
    35–39
  types of, 13–15, 16, 24

what it is, 4–6
autism
  misdiagnosed as ADHD, 29

B

behavioral approaches
  to treating ADHD, 27, 31,
    33, 35, 38–39
boys
  and higher incidence of
    ADHD, 27, 32–33
brain chemistry, 23
brain development, 12–13

C

careers, 90
chores, 57, 59, 86
coexisting conditions
  of ADHD, 32, 40
  college
  and ADHD, 86–87, 89
  combined representation
  of ADHD, 13, 16
community college, 87, 89
concentration
  difficulty with, 4, 7, 13,
    29, 38, 65, 67
Concerta XL, 36
conduct disorder (CD),
  32–33, 46
Crichton, Alexander, 18

ABOUT THE AUTHOR

Dr. Nicki Peter Petrikowski is a literary scholar as well as an editor, author, and translator.

PHOTO CREDITS

Cover, p. 1 © iStockphoto.com/pink_cotton_candy; p. 5 © iStockphoto.com/MickyWiswedel; pp. 8–9 Yellow Dog Productions/The Image Bank/Getty Images; pp. 10–11 Indeed/Getty Images; pp. 14–15 ColorBlind Images/The Image Bank/Getty Images; p. 19 Science Source; pp. 20–21 Culture Club/Hulton Archive/Getty Images; pp. 24–25 UpperCut Images/Getty Images; p. 28 kali9/iStock/Thinkstock; pp. 30–31 Maica/E+/Getty Images; pp. 34–35 Alina Solovyova-Vincent/E+/Getty Images; p. 37 Tracy Dominey/Science Source; pp. 42–43 1MoreCreative/E+/Getty Images; pp. 44–45 Sawayasu Tsuji/E+/Getty Images; p. 48 Martin Novak/Shutterstock.com; pp. 50–51 © iStockphoto.com/Aldo Murillo; pp. 52–53, 56–57, 74–75 Hero Images/Getty Images; p. 58 Tetra Images/Getty Images; pp. 62–63 John Giustina/The Image Bank/Getty Images; pp. 66–67 Creatas Images/Thinkstock; pp. 70–71 Thomas Grass/The Image Bank/Getty Images; pp. 76–77 Fuse/Thinkstock; pp. 78–79 AntonioDiaz/Shutterstock.com; pp. 82–83 © iStockphoto.com/Wavebreak; pp. 84–85 Andresr/Shutterstock.com; pp. 88–89 Ian Jeffery/E+/Getty Images; pp. 92–93 © iStockphoto.com/igenkin.

Designer: Les Kanturek; Editor: Nicholas Croce